WRESTLING TRAINING
LOGBOOK

This book belongs to

_____

_____

_____

Date		Weeks		Time	
Coach				Start	
Hours Trained				End	

GOALS

WARM UP / DRILLS

TECHNIQUE-1

TECHNIQUE-2

NOTES

Date		Weeks		Time	
Coach				Start	
Hours Trained				End	

GOALS

WARM UP / DRILLS

TECHNIQUE-1

TECHNIQUE-2

NOTES

Date		Weeks		Time	
Coach				Start	
Hours Trained				End	

GOALS

WARM UP / DRILLS

TECHNIQUE - 1

TECHNIQUE - 2

NOTES

Date		Weeks		Time	
Coach				Start	
Hours Trained				End	

GOALS

WARM UP / DRILLS

TECHNIQUE-1

TECHNIQUE-2

NOTES

Date		Weeks		Time	
Coach				Start	
Hours Trained				End	

GOALS

WARM UP / DRILLS

TECHNIQUE-1

TECHNIQUE-2

NOTES

Date		Weeks		Time	
Coach				Start	
Hours Trained				End	

GOALS

WARM UP / DRILLS

TECHNIQUE-1

TECHNIQUE-2

NOTES

Date		Weeks		Time	
Coach				Start	
Hours Trained				End	

GOALS

WARM UP / DRILLS

TECHNIQUE- 1

TECHNIQUE- 2

NOTES

Date		Weeks		Time	
Coach				Start	
Hours Trained				End	

GOALS

WARM UP / DRILLS

TECHNIQUE- 1

TECHNIQUE- 2

NOTES

Date		Weeks		Time	
Coach				Start	
Hours Trained				End	

GOALS

WARM UP / DRILLS

TECHNIQUE-1

TECHNIQUE-2

NOTES

Date		Weeks		Time	
Coach				Start	
Hours Trained				End	

GOALS

WARM UP / DRILLS

TECHNIQUE-1

TECHNIQUE-2

NOTES

Date		Weeks		Time	
Coach				Start	
Hours Trained				End	

GOALS

WARM UP / DRILLS

TECHNIQUE-1

TECHNIQUE-2

NOTES

Date		Weeks		Time	
Coach				Start	
Hours Trained				End	

GOALS

WARM UP / DRILLS

TECHNIQUE-1

TECHNIQUE-2

NOTES

Date		Weeks		Time	
Coach				Start	
Hours Trained				End	

GOALS

WARM UP / DRILLS

TECHNIQUE- 1

TECHNIQUE- 2

NOTES

Date		Weeks		Time	
Coach				Start	
Hours Trained				End	

GOALS

WARM UP / DRILLS

TECHNIQUE- 1

TECHNIQUE- 2

NOTES

Date		Weeks		Time	
Coach				Start	
Hours Trained				End	

GOALS

WARM UP / DRILLS

TECHNIQUE-1

TECHNIQUE-2

NOTES

Date		Weeks		Time	
Coach				Start	
Hours Trained				End	

GOALS

WARM UP / DRILLS

TECHNIQUE- 1

TECHNIQUE- 2

NOTES

Date		Weeks		Time	
Coach				Start	
Hours Trained				End	

GOALS

WARM UP / DRILLS

TECHNIQUE-1

TECHNIQUE-2

NOTES

Date		Weeks		Time	
Coach				Start	
Hours Trained				End	

GOALS

WARM UP / DRILLS

TECHNIQUE-1

TECHNIQUE-2

NOTES

Date		Weeks		Time	
Coach				Start	
Hours Trained				End	

GOALS

WARM UP / DRILLS

TECHNIQUE-1

TECHNIQUE-2

NOTES

Date		Weeks		Time	
Coach				Start	
Hours Trained				End	

GOALS

WARM UP / DRILLS

TECHNIQUE- 1

TECHNIQUE- 2

NOTES

Date		Weeks		Time	
Coach				Start	
Hours Trained				End	

GOALS

WARM UP / DRILLS

TECHNIQUE- 1

TECHNIQUE- 2

NOTES

Date		Weeks		Time	
Coach				Start	
Hours Trained				End	

GOALS

WARM UP / DRILLS

TECHNIQUE- 1

TECHNIQUE- 2

NOTES

Date		Weeks		Time	
Coach				Start	
Hours Trained				End	

GOALS

WARM UP / DRILLS

TECHNIQUE-1

TECHNIQUE-2

NOTES

Date		Weeks		Time	
Coach				Start	
Hours Trained				End	

GOALS

WARM UP / DRILLS

TECHNIQUE-1

TECHNIQUE-2

NOTES

Date		Weeks		Time	
Coach				Start	
Hours Trained				End	

GOALS

WARM UP / DRILLS

TECHNIQUE-1

TECHNIQUE-2

NOTES

Date		Weeks		Time	
Coach				Start	
Hours Trained				End	

GOALS

WARM UP / DRILLS

TECHNIQUE-1

TECHNIQUE-2

NOTES

Date		Weeks		Time	
Coach				Start	
Hours Trained				End	

GOALS

WARM UP / DRILLS

TECHNIQUE-1

TECHNIQUE-2

NOTES

Date		Weeks		Time	
Coach				Start	
Hours Trained				End	

GOALS

WARM UP / DRILLS

TECHNIQUE-1

TECHNIQUE-2

NOTES

Date		Weeks		Time	
Coach				Start	
Hours Trained				End	

GOALS

WARM UP / DRILLS

TECHNIQUE- 1

TECHNIQUE- 2

NOTES

Date		Weeks		Time	
Coach				Start	
Hours Trained				End	

GOALS

WARM UP / DRILLS

TECHNIQUE-1

TECHNIQUE-2

NOTES

Date		Weeks		Time	
Coach				Start	
Hours Trained				End	

GOALS

WARM UP / DRILLS

TECHNIQUE- 1

TECHNIQUE- 2

NOTES

Date		Weeks		Time	
Coach				Start	
Hours Trained				End	

GOALS

WARM UP / DRILLS

TECHNIQUE- 1

TECHNIQUE- 2

NOTES

Date		Weeks		Time	
Coach				Start	
Hours Trained				End	

GOALS

WARM UP / DRILLS

TECHNIQUE- 1

TECHNIQUE- 2

NOTES

Date		Weeks		Time	
Coach				Start	
Hours Trained				End	

GOALS

WARM UP / DRILLS

TECHNIQUE-1

TECHNIQUE-2

NOTES

Date		Weeks		Time	
Coach				Start	
Hours Trained				End	

GOALS

WARM UP / DRILLS

TECHNIQUE-1

TECHNIQUE-2

NOTES

Date		Weeks		Time	
Coach				Start	
Hours Trained				End	

GOALS

WARM UP / DRILLS

TECHNIQUE-1

TECHNIQUE-2

NOTES

Date		Weeks		Time	
Coach				Start	
Hours Trained				End	

GOALS

WARM UP / DRILLS

TECHNIQUE-1

TECHNIQUE-2

NOTES

Date		Weeks		Time	
Coach				Start	
Hours Trained				End	

GOALS

WARM UP / DRILLS

TECHNIQUE-1

TECHNIQUE-2

NOTES

Date		Weeks		Time	
Coach				Start	
Hours Trained				End	

GOALS

WARM UP / DRILLS

TECHNIQUE-1

TECHNIQUE-2

NOTES

Date		Weeks		Time	
Coach				Start	
Hours Trained				End	

GOALS

WARM UP / DRILLS

TECHNIQUE-1

TECHNIQUE-2

NOTES

Date		Weeks		Time	
Coach				Start	
Hours Trained				End	

GOALS

WARM UP / DRILLS

TECHNIQUE-1

TECHNIQUE-2

NOTES

Date		Weeks		Time	
Coach				Start	
Hours Trained				End	

GOALS

WARM UP / DRILLS

TECHNIQUE-1

TECHNIQUE-2

NOTES

Date		Weeks		Time	
Coach				Start	
Hours Trained				End	

GOALS

WARM UP / DRILLS

TECHNIQUE-1

TECHNIQUE-2

NOTES

Date		Weeks		Time	
Coach				Start	
Hours Trained				End	

GOALS

WARM UP / DRILLS

TECHNIQUE- 1

TECHNIQUE- 2

NOTES

Date		Weeks		Time	
Coach				Start	
Hours Trained				End	

GOALS

WARM UP / DRILLS

TECHNIQUE-1

TECHNIQUE-2

NOTES

Date		Weeks		Time	
Coach				Start	
Hours Trained				End	

GOALS

WARM UP / DRILLS

TECHNIQUE-1

TECHNIQUE-2

NOTES

Date		Weeks		Time	
Coach				Start	
Hours Trained				End	

GOALS

WARM UP / DRILLS

TECHNIQUE-1

TECHNIQUE-2

NOTES

Date		Weeks		Time	
Coach				Start	
Hours Trained				End	

GOALS

WARM UP / DRILLS

TECHNIQUE-1

TECHNIQUE-2

NOTES

Date		Weeks		Time	
Coach				Start	
Hours Trained				End	

GOALS

WARM UP / DRILLS

TECHNIQUE- 1

TECHNIQUE- 2

NOTES

Date		Weeks		Time	
Coach				Start	
Hours Trained				End	

GOALS

WARM UP / DRILLS

TECHNIQUE - 1

TECHNIQUE - 2

NOTES

Date		Weeks		Time	
Coach				Start	
Hours Trained				End	

GOALS

WARM UP / DRILLS

TECHNIQUE-1

TECHNIQUE-2

NOTES

Date		Weeks		Time	
Coach				Start	
Hours Trained				End	

GOALS

WARM UP / DRILLS

TECHNIQUE-1

TECHNIQUE-2

NOTES

Date		Weeks		Time	
Coach				Start	
Hours Trained				End	

GOALS

WARM UP / DRILLS

TECHNIQUE- 1

TECHNIQUE- 2

NOTES

Date		Weeks		Time	
Coach				Start	
Hours Trained				End	

GOALS

WARM UP / DRILLS

TECHNIQUE-1

TECHNIQUE-2

NOTES

Date		Weeks		Time	
Coach				Start	
Hours Trained				End	

GOALS

WARM UP / DRILLS

TECHNIQUE-1

TECHNIQUE-2

NOTES

Date		Weeks		Time	
Coach				Start	
Hours Trained				End	

GOALS

WARM UP / DRILLS

TECHNIQUE-1

TECHNIQUE-2

NOTES

Date		Weeks		Time	
Coach				Start	
Hours Trained				End	

GOALS

WARM UP / DRILLS

TECHNIQUE-1

TECHNIQUE-2

NOTES

Date		Weeks		Time	
Coach				Start	
Hours Trained				End	

GOALS

WARM UP / DRILLS

TECHNIQUE-1

TECHNIQUE-2

NOTES

Date		Weeks		Time	
Coach				Start	
Hours Trained				End	

GOALS

WARM UP / DRILLS

TECHNIQUE-1

TECHNIQUE-2

NOTES

Date		Weeks		Time	
Coach				Start	
Hours Trained				End	

GOALS

WARM UP / DRILLS

TECHNIQUE- 1

TECHNIQUE- 2

NOTES

Date		Weeks		Time	
Coach				Start	
Hours Trained				End	

GOALS

WARM UP / DRILLS

TECHNIQUE- 1

TECHNIQUE- 2

NOTES

Date		Weeks		Time	
Coach				Start	
Hours Trained				End	

GOALS

WARM UP / DRILLS

TECHNIQUE-1

TECHNIQUE-2

NOTES

Date		Weeks		Time	
Coach				Start	
Hours Trained				End	

GOALS

WARM UP / DRILLS

TECHNIQUE- 1

TECHNIQUE- 2

NOTES

Date		Weeks		Time	
Coach				Start	
Hours Trained				End	

GOALS

WARM UP / DRILLS

TECHNIQUE-1

TECHNIQUE-2

NOTES

Date		Weeks		Time	
Coach				Start	
Hours Trained				End	

GOALS

WARM UP / DRILLS

TECHNIQUE-1

TECHNIQUE-2

NOTES

Date		Weeks		Time	
Coach				Start	
Hours Trained				End	

GOALS

WARM UP / DRILLS

TECHNIQUE-1

TECHNIQUE-2

NOTES

Date		Weeks		Time	
Coach				Start	
Hours Trained				End	

GOALS

WARM UP / DRILLS

TECHNIQUE-1

TECHNIQUE-2

NOTES

Date		Weeks		Time	
Coach				Start	
Hours Trained				End	

GOALS

WARM UP / DRILLS

TECHNIQUE-1

TECHNIQUE-2

NOTES

Date		Weeks		Time	
Coach				Start	
Hours Trained				End	

GOALS

WARM UP / DRILLS

TECHNIQUE-1

TECHNIQUE-2

NOTES

Date		Weeks		Time	
Coach				Start	
Hours Trained				End	

GOALS

WARM UP / DRILLS

TECHNIQUE-1

TECHNIQUE-2

NOTES

Date		Weeks		Time	
Coach				Start	
Hours Trained				End	

GOALS

WARM UP / DRILLS

TECHNIQUE-1

TECHNIQUE-2

NOTES

Date		Weeks		Time	
Coach				Start	
Hours Trained				End	

GOALS

WARM UP / DRILLS

TECHNIQUE-1

TECHNIQUE-2

NOTES

Date		Weeks		Time	
Coach				Start	
Hours Trained				End	

GOALS

WARM UP / DRILLS

TECHNIQUE- 1

TECHNIQUE- 2

NOTES

Date		Weeks		Time	
Coach				Start	
Hours Trained				End	

GOALS

WARM UP / DRILLS

TECHNIQUE-1

TECHNIQUE-2

NOTES

Date		Weeks		Time	
Coach				Start	
Hours Trained				End	

GOALS

WARM UP / DRILLS

TECHNIQUE-1

TECHNIQUE-2

NOTES

Date		Weeks		Time	
Coach				Start	
Hours Trained				End	

GOALS

WARM UP / DRILLS

TECHNIQUE-1

TECHNIQUE-2

NOTES

Date		Weeks		Time	
Coach				Start	
Hours Trained				End	

GOALS

WARM UP / DRILLS

TECHNIQUE-1

TECHNIQUE-2

NOTES

Date		Weeks		Time	
Coach				Start	
Hours Trained				End	

GOALS

WARM UP / DRILLS

TECHNIQUE-1

TECHNIQUE-2

NOTES

Date		Weeks		Time	
Coach				Start	
Hours Trained				End	

GOALS

WARM UP / DRILLS

TECHNIQUE-1

TECHNIQUE-2

NOTES

Date		Weeks		Time	
Coach				Start	
Hours Trained				End	

GOALS

WARM UP / DRILLS

TECHNIQUE-1

TECHNIQUE-2

NOTES

Date		Weeks		Time	
Coach				Start	
Hours Trained				End	

GOALS

WARM UP / DRILLS

TECHNIQUE- 1

TECHNIQUE- 2

NOTES

Date		Weeks		Time	
Coach				Start	
Hours Trained				End	

GOALS

WARM UP / DRILLS

TECHNIQUE-1

TECHNIQUE-2

NOTES

Date		Weeks		Time	
Coach				Start	
Hours Trained				End	

GOALS

WARM UP / DRILLS

TECHNIQUE-1

TECHNIQUE-2

NOTES

Date		Weeks		Time	
Coach				Start	
Hours Trained				End	

GOALS

WARM UP / DRILLS

TECHNIQUE-1

TECHNIQUE-2

NOTES

Date		Weeks		Time	
Coach				Start	
Hours Trained				End	

GOALS

WARM UP / DRILLS

TECHNIQUE-1

TECHNIQUE-2

NOTES

Date		Weeks		Time	
Coach				Start	
Hours Trained				End	

GOALS

WARM UP / DRILLS

TECHNIQUE-1

TECHNIQUE-2

NOTES

Date		Weeks		Time	
Coach				Start	
Hours Trained				End	

GOALS

WARM UP / DRILLS

TECHNIQUE-1

TECHNIQUE-2

NOTES

Date		Weeks		Time	
Coach				Start	
Hours Trained				End	

GOALS

WARM UP / DRILLS

TECHNIQUE-1

TECHNIQUE-2

NOTES

Date		Weeks		Time	
Coach				Start	
Hours Trained				End	

GOALS

WARM UP / DRILLS

TECHNIQUE- 1

TECHNIQUE- 2

NOTES

Date		Weeks		Time	
Coach				Start	
Hours Trained				End	

GOALS

WARM UP / DRILLS

TECHNIQUE-1

TECHNIQUE-2

NOTES

Date		Weeks		Time	
Coach				Start	
Hours Trained				End	

GOALS

WARM UP / DRILLS

TECHNIQUE-1

TECHNIQUE-2

NOTES

Date		Weeks		Time	
Coach				Start	
Hours Trained				End	

GOALS

WARM UP / DRILLS

TECHNIQUE-1

TECHNIQUE-2

NOTES

Date		Weeks		Time	
Coach				Start	
Hours Trained				End	

GOALS

WARM UP / DRILLS

TECHNIQUE-1

TECHNIQUE-2

NOTES

Date		Weeks		Time	
Coach				Start	
Hours Trained				End	

GOALS

WARM UP / DRILLS

TECHNIQUE-1

TECHNIQUE-2

NOTES

Date		Weeks		Time	
Coach				Start	
Hours Trained				End	

GOALS

WARM UP / DRILLS

TECHNIQUE- 1

TECHNIQUE- 2

NOTES

Date		Weeks		Time	
Coach				Start	
Hours Trained				End	

GOALS

WARM UP / DRILLS

TECHNIQUE-1

TECHNIQUE-2

NOTES

Date		Weeks		Time	
Coach				Start	
Hours Trained				End	

GOALS

WARM UP / DRILLS

TECHNIQUE- 1

TECHNIQUE- 2

NOTES

Date		Weeks		Time	
Coach				Start	
Hours Trained				End	

GOALS

WARM UP / DRILLS

TECHNIQUE-1

TECHNIQUE-2

NOTES

Date		Weeks		Time	
Coach				Start	
Hours Trained				End	

GOALS

WARM UP / DRILLS

TECHNIQUE-1

TECHNIQUE-2

NOTES

Date		Weeks		Time	
Coach				Start	
Hours Trained				End	

GOALS

WARM UP / DRILLS

TECHNIQUE-1

TECHNIQUE-2

NOTES

Date		Weeks		Time	
Coach				Start	
Hours Trained				End	

GOALS

WARM UP / DRILLS

TECHNIQUE- 1

TECHNIQUE- 2

NOTES

Date		Weeks		Time	
Coach				Start	
Hours Trained				End	

GOALS

WARM UP / DRILLS

TECHNIQUE-1

TECHNIQUE-2

NOTES

Date		Weeks		Time	
Coach				Start	
Hours Trained				End	

GOALS

WARM UP / DRILLS

TECHNIQUE-1

TECHNIQUE-2

NOTES

Date		Weeks		Time	
Coach				Start	
Hours Trained				End	

GOALS

WARM UP / DRILLS

TECHNIQUE-1

TECHNIQUE-2

NOTES

Date		Weeks		Time	
Coach				Start	
Hours Trained				End	

GOALS

WARM UP / DRILLS

TECHNIQUE-1

TECHNIQUE-2

NOTES

Date		Weeks		Time	
Coach				Start	
Hours Trained				End	

GOALS

WARM UP / DRILLS

TECHNIQUE-1

TECHNIQUE-2

NOTES

Date		Weeks		Time	
Coach				Start	
Hours Trained				End	

GOALS

WARM UP / DRILLS

TECHNIQUE-1

TECHNIQUE-2

NOTES

Date		Weeks		Time	
Coach				Start	
Hours Trained				End	

GOALS

WARM UP / DRILLS

TECHNIQUE-1

TECHNIQUE-2

NOTES

Date		Weeks		Time	
Coach				Start	
Hours Trained				End	

GOALS

WARM UP / DRILLS

TECHNIQUE-1

TECHNIQUE-2

NOTES

Date		Weeks		Time	
Coach				Start	
Hours Trained				End	

GOALS

WARM UP / DRILLS

TECHNIQUE-1

TECHNIQUE-2

NOTES

Date		Weeks		Time	
Coach				Start	
Hours Trained				End	

GOALS

WARM UP / DRILLS

TECHNIQUE-1

TECHNIQUE-2

NOTES

Date		Weeks		Time	
Coach				Start	
Hours Trained				End	

GOALS

WARM UP / DRILLS

TECHNIQUE-1

TECHNIQUE-2

NOTES

Date		Weeks		Time	
Coach				Start	
Hours Trained				End	

GOALS

WARM UP / DRILLS

TECHNIQUE-1

TECHNIQUE-2

NOTES

Date		Weeks		Time	
Coach				Start	
Hours Trained				End	

GOALS

WARM UP / DRILLS

TECHNIQUE- 1

TECHNIQUE- 2

NOTES

Date		Weeks		Time	
Coach				Start	
Hours Trained				End	

GOALS

WARM UP / DRILLS

TECHNIQUE-1

TECHNIQUE-2

NOTES

Date		Weeks		Time	
Coach				Start	
Hours Trained				End	

GOALS

WARM UP / DRILLS

TECHNIQUE- 1

TECHNIQUE- 2

NOTES

Date		Weeks		Time	
Coach				Start	
Hours Trained				End	

GOALS

WARM UP / DRILLS

TECHNIQUE-1

TECHNIQUE-2

NOTES

Date		Weeks		Time	
Coach				Start	
Hours Trained				End	

GOALS

WARM UP / DRILLS

TECHNIQUE-1

TECHNIQUE-2

NOTES

Date		Weeks		Time	
Coach				Start	
Hours Trained				End	

GOALS

WARM UP / DRILLS

TECHNIQUE-1

TECHNIQUE-2

NOTES

Date		Weeks		Time	
Coach				Start	
Hours Trained				End	

GOALS

WARM UP / DRILLS

TECHNIQUE-1

TECHNIQUE-2

NOTES

Date		Weeks		Time	
Coach				Start	
Hours Trained				End	

GOALS

WARM UP / DRILLS

TECHNIQUE-1

TECHNIQUE-2

NOTES

Date		Weeks		Time	
Coach				Start	
Hours Trained				End	

GOALS

WARM UP / DRILLS

TECHNIQUE-1

TECHNIQUE-2

NOTES

Date		Weeks		Time	
Coach				Start	
Hours Trained				End	

GOALS

WARM UP / DRILLS

TECHNIQUE-1

TECHNIQUE-2

NOTES

Date		Weeks		Time	
Coach				Start	
Hours Trained				End	

GOALS

WARM UP / DRILLS

TECHNIQUE-1

TECHNIQUE-2

NOTES

Date		Weeks		Time	
Coach				Start	
Hours Trained				End	

GOALS

WARM UP / DRILLS

TECHNIQUE-1

TECHNIQUE-2

NOTES

Date		Weeks		Time	
Coach				Start	
Hours Trained				End	

GOALS

WARM UP / DRILLS

TECHNIQUE-1

TECHNIQUE-2

NOTES

Date		Weeks		Time	
Coach				Start	
Hours Trained				End	

GOALS

WARM UP / DRILLS

TECHNIQUE-1

TECHNIQUE-2

NOTES

Date		Weeks		Time	
Coach				Start	
Hours Trained				End	

GOALS

WARM UP / DRILLS

TECHNIQUE-1

TECHNIQUE-2

NOTES

Date		Weeks		Time	
Coach				Start	
Hours Trained				End	

GOALS

WARM UP / DRILLS

TECHNIQUE- 1

TECHNIQUE- 2

NOTES

Date		Weeks		Time	
Coach				Start	
Hours Trained				End	

GOALS

WARM UP / DRILLS

TECHNIQUE-1

TECHNIQUE-2

NOTES

www.ingramcontent.com/pod-product-compliance
Lightning Source LLC
Chambersburg PA
CBHW081619100526
44590CB00021B/3518